# FROM
# A.D.D.
## TO
# CEO

# FROM
# A.D.D.
# TO
# CEO

## A CEO'S JOURNEY *from* CHAOS *to* SUCCESS

· ASHTON HARRISON ·

www.ADDtoCEO.com

Published by Advantage, Charleston, South Carolina.
Member of Advantage Media Group.

ADVANTAGE is a registered trademark and the Advantage colophon is a trademark of Advantage Media Group, Inc.

Printed in the United States of America.

ISBN: 978-1-59932-000-0
LCCN: 2012949090

This publication is designed to provide accurate and authoritative information in regard to the subject matter covered. It is sold with the understanding that the publisher is not engaged in rendering legal, accounting, or other professional services. If legal advice or other expert assistance is required, the services of a competent professional person should be sought.

Advantage Media Group is proud to be a part of the Tree Neutral® program. Tree Neutral offsets the number of trees consumed in the production and printing of this book by taking proactive steps such as planting trees in direct proportion to the number of trees used to print books. To learn more about Tree Neutral, please visit www.treeneutral.com. To learn more about Advantage's commitment to being a responsible steward of the environment, please visit www.advantagefamily.com/green

Advantage Media Group is a leading publisher of business, motivation, and self-help authors. Do you have a manuscript or book idea that you would like to have considered for publication? Please visit www.advantagefamily.com or call 1.866.775.1696

Photography by Marsi Harrison
www.MarsiHarrison.com

*This book is dedicated to my father, Thomas Evan Williams (1921–2010), from whom my siblings and I derived our ADD/CEO bloodline, and to whom I will be forever grateful for his guidance, inspiration, and love.*

This story begins by describing my efforts to cope with the challenges of attention deficit disorder (ADD), but it unfolds to show the rich discoveries that turned my struggle into acceptance of my ADD tendencies. Once I owned up to these traits, I was able to draw strength and great value from them. Whether you are a business manager, an entrepreneur, stay-at-home mom, or community volunteer, you are a CEO. Whether you have ADD or not, you can learn management strategies from ADD to CEO.

# TABLE OF CONTENTS

# Foreword

In this book I share the skills I had to develop and utilize in order to cope with my attention deficit disorder (ADD) challenges and how I learned to maximize my ADD benefits. This book is also intended for anyone who may be in one of those painful and stressful phases of corporate growth on the way to the goalpost. If I had known then what I know now, I think I could have saved myself a lot of stress and achieved my chosen goals many years earlier. Even when I thought I had the right crew onboard, I might have noticed that I did not, if someone had simply painted these pictures for me. The problem with having ADD is that in order to be a successful CEO, you have to have a laser-like focus and the ability to think as straight as an arrow—when, in fact, your attention pattern is shaped more like a squiggle. (Have you ever taken the Personality Shapes quiz: http://www.etals.com/pershape.html)? That's where the strategy coach comes in.

Although this book was written with the CEO in mind, every individual manages something in life and everyone is a CEO of something. If you are in sales, you are the CEO of your own destiny. A stay-at-home mom is CEO of the family. Anyone who manages anything is a CEO, whether it is a company, club, soccer team, or a volunteer group.

My intention is to help you recognize and understand your own ADD strengths and challenges and help "regular people"—whom I will call ABC people—understand you in the process. The quiz in Chapter 1 is designed to help ADD people understand ABC people and vice versa. All of us CEOs with ADD bring so much to an organization in spite of the chaos we tend to create. We are quite driven—at times to distraction—yet very dedicated and determined with a tireless energy and the quick-study brain that others just cannot relate to. However, the ability to see and sense everything tends to constantly trip us up, so it can take us longer to get to the next step.

You may think this book is somewhat brief and a bit scattered, but you can bet that ADD people will follow right along with me. I have attempted to appeal to ADD people with the book's outline form, brief summaries, and to-the-point lists.

Writing this book has helped me—and my husband—better understand how I function. It has helped us recognize my limitations, too. I now think about how I do almost everything, and I use some of my own strategies every day.

# Chapter 1

# Introduction

I am not aware if the question of ADD CEOs has ever been studied in a formal way, but I am fairly confident that many successful entrepreneurs suffer from some ADD. In fact, I would take this theory all the way to the corner office and suggest that many chief executives have ADD symptoms.

We on the ADD side have particular strengths for running companies, especially when they are small. ADD people like me prefer to be in charge because we tend to think and operate idiosyncratically and don't follow rules set by others very well. We are extremely good at multitasking, which helps us to manage the many facets of running a small company. But we are constantly distracted due to acute awareness of our surroundings. ADD often means that you hear and see virtually everything happening in your environment. The ability to multitask enables us to recognize potential problems in a company before they take hold.

ADD types are creative, innovative, and often develop solutions no one else has ever thought of. But often we don't slow down long enough to consider all the consequences of our decisions. My information technology manager's favorite memory of working for me is the day I asked him to redesign our website in two weeks. The process actually took six months. No one ever has to tell people like me to think outside the box because we are already there.

Some of the highest-achieving people in history—athletes, inventors, entertainers, artists, politicians, and business leaders among others—have ADD. From these occasionally scatterbrained people have come great works and feats. Of course, many of their best ideas and projects have not made it to completion. According to studies, 100 percent of this who's-who list is made up of ADD sufferers: Leonardo Da Vinci, Frank Lloyd Wright, Pablo Picasso, Babe Ruth, Magic Johnson, Michael Jordan, Pete Rose, Michael Phelps, Edgar Allen Poe, F. Scott Fitzgerald, Ralph Waldo Emerson, Mozart, Beethoven, Handel, Malcolm Forbes, John D. Rockefeller, William Randolph Hearst, Christopher Columbus, Lewis and Clark, Alexander Graham Bell, Thomas Edison, Newton, Pasteur, Benjamin Franklin, Ansel Adams, Albert Einstein, and Gen. George Patton (http://add.about.com/od/famouspeoplewithadhd/a/famouspeople. htm). Their legacies prove that ADD is not a handicap in the quest to achieve greatness as long as some measure of self-discipline is applied.

ADD people tend to be highly energetic and have trouble sitting down and relaxing. It just seems so "unproductive." We thrive on getting things done. That's why so many ADD people work or volunteer their time rather than seek out downtime. Most people around us tire of watching us and constantly suggest that we relax. Personally, I find it onerous to sit around and do nothing. The word *idle* is just not in my vocabulary.

The ADD brain constantly operates at a higher RPM. Insomnia is a common trait among ADD people. We have trouble falling asleep at night because our brain simply cannot slow down. I have been known to ask my spouse a question and before he can formulate an answer, I have asked him four other questions. Since we naturally operate in permanent multitask mode, we do not single-task very well. "Efficiency" is our motto.

A simple way to understand the ADD brain compared to the ABC brain is to look at the gearshift selector in your car. The ADD brain is always in D (drive or high gear). It rarely slows down, never stops, and certainly does not reverse direction. The ABC brain, on the other hand, is analogous to P-R-N-D-D2. It recognizes when to switch between park and drive, from standard drive to drive 2, or even into reverse. There is a natural ability to analyze and utilize the best gear for the moment. The ADD brain has one gear: go.

*Learn to meditate. This will be extremely hard for you since it requires completely erasing your mind of all thoughts. I focus on a "blank blackboard." Meditation is the only way to quiet our minds (without medication) so that we can fall back asleep.*

No one needs to force us to make decisions. We have already formulated an opinion long before we have all the facts. Details don't really matter to us, as they require additional focus. When we have an opinion, we are most confident that it is right, and we will work hard to defend it. An ADD person would never make a good analyst because that would require patience to gather all the facts and study results carefully before making a decision. We generally act on impulse, often completing projects and goals while others continue researching. This can be both beneficial and detrimental for the executive who makes it up to CEO. Sometimes we are way ahead of the competition and are first with a new product or process. Other times we can take the company down the wrong path on a whim.

The ideal ADD spouse is decidedly not ADD, but offers a calming, organized, balancing effect that can help us slow down, focus, and smell the roses. Such a spouse is owed a debt of gratitude.

The three ADD traits that most irritate my spouse are:

1. **I ask** him additional questions while he is still thinking of the answer to the last one.

2. **I answer** questions other people have asked him because I become impatient as he forms a response.

3. **I create** clutter everywhere I go.

Distracted by new initiatives repeatedly, ADD people can easily go through an entire day and never get to the first item on their list.

This book is not so much about what I did right as what I did wrong or would have done differently, knowing what I know now.

ADD people tend to like and therefore hire other ADD people. What we really need is to surround ourselves with opposite types: the ABC-brained people. My own inclination to hire fellow members of the ADD club caused me major problems. By chance, more than anything, I eventually found myself employing lots of non-ADD staff members. That's when I found I had a staff capable of creating order and executing plans—in other words, a staff that could make my company a success. The hardest thing for an ADD CEO is being willing to admit how bad things really are. But once the ADD CEO does that, things will get better. Two years before we sold our business, I had two different accountants recommend that we liquidate. That would have been financially devastating. Even worse, we would have put 60 employees on the street overnight.

So let's take a look at the characteristics of ADD people, successful CEOs, and successful entrepreneurs to see how they pair up.

## DO YOU HAVE ATTENTION DEFICIT DISORDER?

Take the following quiz to determine if you have ADD:
Count the total number of a's, b's, c's, and d's.

1.  When attacking my to-do list:
    a.  I usually focus on the task at hand until I complete it.
    b.  I often multitask by doing more than two things at the same time, so I get them finished twice as fast as others.
    c.  I do three or more things at the same time, often while driving.
    d.  Which to-do list? I already lost the one I made this morning.

2.  Do you ever interrupt people?
    a.  Never. I always wait my turn to speak and consider it rude to interrupt.
    b.  I try not to interrupt people, but sometimes I forget and feel compelled to express myself.
    c.  I am constantly interrupting people, so I don't forget what I have to say.
    d.  I'm sorry. What was the question? I was in the middle of two other conversations.

3.  How often do you read a book?
    a.  Every chance I can.
    b.  One a month.
    c.  A few books a year, mostly skipping pages.
    d.  Even finishing a newspaper or magazine article is a stretch.

4.  Do you tend to complete a task once you start it?
    a.  I focus on the task until it is complete and finish one task before starting another.
    b.  I sometimes have two to three things going on at once.
    c.  I am a master of multitasking and always have at least 10 projects going on.
    d.  I'll be lucky if I finish this quiz.

5.  Are you on time for appointments?
    a.  I always arrive 15 minutes early.
    b.  I am always on time.
    c.  Occasionally, I am a few minutes late for an appointment.
    d.  Oh drat. I'm supposed to be somewhere right now.

6.  Do you underestimate the time it takes to complete tasks?
    a.  Never. I always research and make a plan so I know how much time I will need.
    b.  Rarely. I usually give myself extra time just in case.
    c.  I tend to underestimate the time but generally finish within a reasonable period.
    d.  On my last large project I budgeted one day's time and it took me three weeks.

7.  How clean do you keep your car?
    a.  Pristine and organized. Everything has a place.
    b.  Pretty organized, though it could use a little spring cleaning.
    c.  I can accommodate another passenger if I rearrange a few things.
    d.  The car wash charges double to clean the inside of my car.

8.  Do you get bored easily and constantly start new things that you know nothing about?
    a.  I do extensive research before starting something new.
    b.  When I see something that inspires me, I will try to pick it up when I have time.
    c.  I have added three new hobbies this month but don't know how to do any of them very well.
    d.  I am in the middle of page four of my bucket list, but I am not following it in order.

9.   How often do you drop your cell phone?
     a.   I have never dropped my cell phone. I keep it safe and secure.
     b.   I drop it on occasion.
     c.   I'm on a first-name basis with the folks at the phone store.
     d.   Oops, my cell phone…Anybody seen my cell phone?

10.  What does your desk look like?
     a.   An organized workspace with everything in its place.
     b.   It has neat stacks of papers.
     c.   It's messy, but I know where everything is.
     d.   It's been so long since I've seen the desktop, I have forgotten what color it is.

11.  Complete this sentence: Before making a decision…
     a.   I calculate all the risks/rewards and analyze the situation.
     b.   I use analysis and intuition equally.
     c.   If it feels right, I tend to go with it.
     d.   I've already made my decision. Can we move on please?

12. Do you have trouble sitting still and paying attention?
    a. I enjoy sitting quietly and have no trouble paying attention for long periods of time.
    b. I can sit still, but my mind sometimes wanders.
    c. After five minutes in a meeting, I am doing at least one other thing as well.
    d. Thank goodness for my cell phone and iPad as they allow me to do several other things while I am in a meeting.

13. When taking a test:
    a. I carefully consider each answer and recheck my answers when done.
    b. I read every word of each question and answer them in order quickly.
    c. I am always one of the first to finish but make some careless mistakes.
    d. Was there a second page to this quiz?

14. After purchasing a new appliance or electronic gadget:
    a. I read the instructions and put it together in order. Then I follow the operating instructions.
    b. I skim the instructions and then follow the proper sequence mostly from memory.
    c. I look at the diagrams and quickly try to put it together without reading the step-by-step instructions. If all else fails, I will consult the manual.
    d. I always have extra pieces and parts that look important.

15. Which of the following describes your driving record?
    a. Clean as a whistle.
    b. Maybe one speeding ticket or fender bender in the past three to five years.
    c. My driving "incidents" in the last three years will still fit on a Post-It note.
    d. I have my attorney's and my insurance agent's numbers on speed dial.

16. Rules are...
    a. Very important for safety and efficiency and keeping order.
    b. Generally appropriate but not always.
    c. Needed for some people.
    d. I make my own rules.

17. Describe your computer screen.
    a. It is clean and all files are in folders.
    b. My computer is clean but the files are a little disorganized.
    c. There are so many files and folders it would make your head spin.
    d. Behind the Post-Its, I'm not sure what you would find.

18. When an invitation arrives:
    a. I always RSVP promptly and arrive on time for the event.
    b. I RSVP right away and try to arrive "fashionably" on time.
    c. When I don't lose the invitation, I RSVP and put it on my calendar.
    d. I have lost at least one invitation in the past year and forgot to attend an event for which I had accepted the invitation or arrived on the wrong day/night.

19. When there is free time:
    a. I sit, relax, and read.
    b. I do a preplanned fun activity.
    c. I fill it with new activities.
    d. What's free time? And I can't sit still anyway.

20. When waiting in line:
    a. I always wait patiently for my turn.
    b. I wait my turn, but I'm irritated by people who butt in line in front of me.
    c. Occasionally, when I am in a hurry, I have been known to butt in line and complain profusely.
    d. Waiting in line is for the other people.

21. When shopping for a major purchase:
    a. I always research online and seek out other opinions before purchasing and always save enough money before making the final purchase.
    b. I will shop online so I know the best price and read the reviews, and then I buy with a credit card.
    c. I use my smartphone to check it out when I first see it but then buy at the first store if I get a reasonable deal.
    d. I want it now. I buy it now.

22. In the kitchen:
    a. I plan meals a week in advance and go to the grocery store once a week. Then I follow my recipes exactly.
    b. I roughly plan meals a few days at a time, and sometimes I will add a little something extra to a recipe.
    c. I come home from work, look in the refrigerator, and throw something together without consulting a recipe.
    d. The kitchen, the refrigerator, and the cupboards are such a mess, I can't figure out how to make dinner. Its 8:30 p.m. and I have not fed my children. Time to call for pizza.

18 or more a's:

You are extremely organized and focused. Maybe even …?

18 or more a + b's:

You fall into the "normal" range of functioning adults.

18 or more b + c's:
You have learned to keep your ADD tendencies in check.

*Use Post-Its to remember appointments, things to do, things to take with you. The inside of an exit door at home, the car dashboard, and the place at work where you leave your keys are all good places for Post-Its.*

18 or more c + d's:
You probably already know that you are ADD.

18 or more d's:

You probably haven't gotten this far anyway.

## CHARACTERISTICS OF ADD PEOPLE AND ENTREPRENEURS

### Generally accepted characteristics of successful CEOs:*

1. Ability to focus on the vision and communicate that vision to stakeholders;
2. Awareness of operational details, though not involved with them;
3. On top of industry trends and known as an avid reader;
4. Hires strong management teams and supports their decisions;
5. Meets with customers and can articulate customer needs, challenges and business goals.

* *Paula Phelan: http://www.nadelphelan.com/*

## Generally accepted characteristics of successful entrepreneurs:*

1. Leadership: ability to build consensus in the face of uncertainty;
2. Communication: ability to send a clear and consistent message;
3. Decision making: knowing when to make a decision;
4. Being a good team player: knowing when to trust and when to delegate;
5. Ability to telescope: focusing on the details before moving back to the bigger picture.

*Jerry Kaplan, Stanford University*

*http://www.academicearth.org/lectures/five-critical-skills-that-entrepreneurs-need*

## My own characteristics of successful entrepreneurs:

1. Driven; make sure every detail gets addressed; read and research everything in the field.
2. A record of winning, in athletics, volunteer work, leadership positions and the like; won't give up until they win.
3. Intelligent and intuitive.
4. Strong left brain to handle logical, analytic, objective thinking, plus a strong right brain for creativity and intuitive feel; (entrepreneurs who lack strong left and right brains will need a partner, be it a CFO, chief of design, or other type of right-hand person, but he or she must be a high-level executive or even a co-owner).
5. Willing to constantly and honestly evaluate competitive advantages and the business's value proposition.
6. Able to face reality even when it's bad and then admit mistakes and fix them; never blame economic factors or other people.

7. Earned some income by age 16.
8. Extremely self-disciplined; skilled at time-management and goal-setting.
9. Sense of responsibility to self and others.
10. Courageous and willing to take a risk.
11. Resilient.
12. Passion for the activity and natural ability to lead and inspire.
13. Limitless energy.
14. Focus on the big picture.
15. Desire to "keep score".
16. High self-expectations.
17. Willing to learn from others and open to others' ideas.
18. Inquisitive nature, especially for learning why and what customers buy, how employees view their work and how decisions are made.
19. Inspire others to follow them, based on their ability to be encouraging, positive, honest, logical, and good communicators (for ideas, see http://www.appleseeds.org/10-inspire_Angier.htm).
20. Willing to confront people in situations such as negotiating expenses, employee performance, etc.

The good news is that we ADDs have the energy, vision, multi-tasking ability, drive, willingness to take risks, and intuition to really get a company off the ground. The bad news is the focus, organization, discipline, and patience needed to grow a company can be a challenge for most ADD managers.

*Set aside time every day to get organized. Use technology to help you stay organized. If you lose your phone or keys, there is a gizmo you can get that beeps if your phone is separated from your keys. Smart phones and iPads really can help an ADD person.*

## WHO AM I?

I am the second child in a family of four children. My father, grandfather, brother, and several uncles all started and sold their own businesses. When I was growing up, ADD had not been identified and labeled. We did not know it at the time, but my father, two sisters, and brother were all affected by ADD. Our family was always on the go and our house was constantly full of activity and noise. All our friends could be found at our house because there was always something fun going on. We had a ski house with four bedrooms and most weekends we had 20 or more people staying there. Somehow my parents managed to feed everyone (and control the chaos?). I remember going to my friends' houses and finding them so quiet they felt like ghost towns. I always thought that I had to whisper when I was visiting because everything was so quiet.

It was only when my sister's child was having trouble in school that I first heard of ADD. One day my sister Lacy showed me a report on her son that included statements such as "he has trouble focusing in the classroom," and "he could do much better if he paid attention to the teacher rather than looking out of the window." She took him for an evaluation and they diagnosed him with ADD. I remember the two of us reading the list of ADD characteristics and realizing that it described us as well. We asked each other, "So they call this a disability?" We realized that our entire family was affected by ADD and most of our children had ADD also. Years later we found some of my grade-school report cards. Anyone could diagnose me with ADD just by reading the teachers' comments.

Having ADD, I start lots of projects and never finish them. My desk has always been a disaster, but I know where everything is, and I constantly amaze people by quickly finding a needed piece of paper.

Keep only one to-do list and train yourself to keep it with you at all times. If you use paper, keep the pad on your desk attached in a special place or at the bottom of your computer screen. But even better is to use smartphone technology for this list. Then prioritize and use asterisks to indicate the subset of tasks that is reasonable to finish in that day. Keep your grocery list and gift ideas on your smartphone as well.

ADD people are not attentive drivers. We are easily distracted. Our attention strays here and there as we drive along. This was a problem even before cell phones. Our impatience results in more than our share of speeding tickets. My father lost his driver's license for an entire year because he had so many speeding tickets. He had to hire a driver to ferry him around. As a teenager, when my siblings and I received speeding tickets or incurred fender benders, our father was most understanding because he had more driving incidents than all of us put together. I pity the poor insurance company that insured our family. Then there was the time my ADD daughter and I were driving separate cars and collided in our driveway. Both cars had to be towed away. I was, of course, dialing my cell phone at the time. My teenage daughter never admitted to me what she was doing.

Clutter seems to follow me wherever I go: in my car, on the kitchen counter, on my desk, in my sewing room, in my bedroom. Even my purse contains so much clutter that I won a scavenger hunt just with items from my purse.

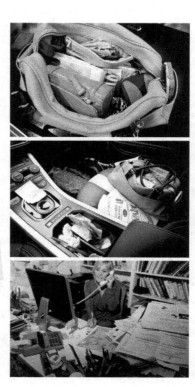

Set up one "mess room" with wall-to-wall shelves to hold all your projects, clutter, reading material, and other things you think you need. Find an unencumbered space elsewhere that will be for work only, not storage. Collect what you need from the mess room, bring it to the clean, bare workspace. Do your work, and then return all materials to your junk room. Don't let your spouse in this room. If your office looks like mine, train your assistant to escort all clients to your conference room, or any other comfortable area from which no one can see your desk.

When my ABC husband bought a large powerboat, he researched boats for years online and in magazines. He had conversations with hundreds of boat owners. He attended the Annapolis and Fort Lauderdale powerboat shows, staring at hundreds of boats to determine the make and model that best fit his needs and preferences. Then he traveled up and down the East Coast looking at the particular model of boat he had decided to buy. He took boating courses to learn how to captain boats and how to navigate. When he finally found a great value, he bought his boat. Contrast that with my ADD father making a substantial purchase. Dad lived in Richmond, Virginia, and worked in Leesburg, Virginia, which was at least a two-hour drive. One day a friend said to him, "Tom, with all this driving you do, you should have a plane." He had never flown a plane, but he bought one the next day. The plane came with flying lessons, as he explained to my mother.

Like so many other ADD entrepreneurs, I got an early start. At 16 years of age I operated a summer playschool in my parents' basement. I had two other friends who drove the pick-up and delivery service, plus three younger helpers with me in the basement. This earned me spending money all through college. I attended three colleges but still managed to finish in four years. It took me five years of part-time study to earn my MBA, but I always came out with impressive grades, much to the surprise of more than one professor. With a degree in elementary education, I taught school for two years and then went to work in a business so I could someday start my own. I was fortunate to be hired by a young and growing company, This End Up Furniture, which I remained with for nine years as it grew from seven retail stores to 100. When I left the company, its annual sales were up to $40 million. I learned every aspect of the operation, from accounting to retailing to management, and ended up as vice president with some equity shares that provided me seed money to start my own company in 1986.

That quick bit of history brings us to the story of my business, Shades of Light.

During my time with This End Up Furniture, I took note of the superior lighting at the wholesale markets, lighting not sold in local retail stores. I started Shades of Light as a lighting and lampshade store, catering to decorators and high-end consumers who were looking for more style-oriented merchandise than traditional builders' showrooms carried. Shades of Light carried table lamps, floor lamps, chandeliers, wall sconces, bath lights, ceiling lights, outdoor lighting, picture lights, ceiling medallions, pendants, and mirrors. My idea was to have a niche market that no one else was covering. As time went on, we expanded to antique lighting, ceiling fans, rugs, accent furniture, and home accessories. We started with one retail store and over time added two more, one of them a liquidation center for discontinued merchandise. We also launched a national mail-order catalog and a website. One-fourth of our current product selection is our own exclusive designs, an advantage in terms of higher margins and more competitive retail prices.

Shades of Light was run according to this mission statement: *Always thrill the customer with unique products, incomparable service, and superior expertise.*

## Shades of Light Timeline:

1986  First store opened in Richmond, Virginia,
      in the back of a building.

1987  Store moved across the street to a more visible space.

1989  Took over space next door to double
      size of store to 4000 square feet.

1993  Moved back across street to take over the entire main
      floor of the building where we had started out, an
      8,000-square-foot space; purchased the building, as well.

1995  Started the Shades of Light catalog
      and mailed 150,000 copies.

1997  Started www.ShadesOfLight.com.

1999  Added accent rugs to catalog.

2001  Moved retail store and offices to a 15,000-square-
      foot building purchased for the same price
      the original building sold for.

2003  Opened an outlet store in Richmond, Virginia.

2006  Moved the outlet store.

2007  Opened a Virginia Beach retail location.

2008  Moved our warehouse, purchasing the building we moved to.

2011  Sold the business.

## Awards won by Shades of Light:

1993   Small Business Entrepreneur of the Year finalist

1994   Small Business Entrepreneur of the Year finalist

2002   Rug Retailer of the Year (America's Mart)

2002   Arts Award: Eastern Lighting Showroom

2003   Consumer Catalogue of the Year
       (Catalog Success Magazine)

2003   Arts Award: Consumer cataloger of the Year

2003   Impact Award Finalist (Community Spirit)

2004   Ernst & Young Entrepreneur finalist

2010   Showroom of the Year Finalist (Dallas Market Center)

# Chapter 2

# How I Made It from ADD to CEO

M any ADD people become CEOs because they are creative and willing to task a risk in starting their own businesses. ADD people like to be the boss. We are leaders rather than followers. Our brains work in a way that lets us see it all—the forest as well as the trees. We also love to multitask. These traits make us natural leaders.

So how do you get out of the forest and see the big picture when you need to? How do you bring a sense of order and accountability to your company? How do you force yourself to focus long enough to endure long meetings, goal-setting sessions, and brainstorming roundtables? How do you find the patience to analyze results and possible strategies? How do you learn to listen to other people and work collaboratively in a team environment? It's a big challenge, but it can be done. You really can start off as a bouncing-off-walls ADD person, and actually end up an effective CEO. I'm confident I can shed some light on the process.

When I first started my company, I was the typical ADD person, doing everything and jetting from one thing to another. I had to learn to delegate, manage my employees, and focus on the big picture:

top-line revenues and bottom-line profits. The same traits that caused me to lose focus also helped me become a successful CEO. These unique ADD characteristics helped me run my company, sometimes effectively and sometimes ineffectively, but that's the batting average of almost every chief executive. Consider these characteristics:

1. An ability to see and hear everything: ADD people are said to have eyes in the back of their heads. We see and hear what's happening all around us. When my husband and I go out to dinner, I hear all the conversations at the tables around me. I will often mention to my husband something about the conversation at the next table, and he has no idea what I am talking about. One day, while working at This End Up, I noticed smoke outside the window. None of the other employees noticed it, even though we were working in the same room. I impulsively ordered everyone to grab their purses, get the computer backups, and get out of the building immediately. Minutes later we learned that our building had caught fire from an adjacent warehouse. The computer back-up tapes allowed us to continue business within a few days. This ability to be distracted by everything around me may in this case have saved lives.

2. Multitasking, aka shifting from one incomplete task to another: It will drive an ADD person's spouse crazy and cause the ADD person's desk to resemble a war zone, but the ability to multitask is helpful for addressing the millions of problems that arise each day if you're running a business. The challenge of the ADD person is to not get caught up in every detail, to be able to come back to the big picture

and the really important things, and to delegate or postpone the less important tasks. I used my "Three things I must do TODAY" list in the early days and later changed it to "Three employee/goal meetings I must accomplish before I leave today." This gave me the discipline I needed to actually get to the important matters. ADD multitasking is often misunderstood by ABC people. My CFO's most amusing memory of my ADD modus operandi goes like this: "We had a FedEx meeting in your office to talk about pricing and you were working away on your computer and we couldn't even tell you were paying attention. Then, you swiveled around in your chair and set them straight on what you wanted from them. It took us all by surprise, but you were spot on. The look on their faces was priceless."

3. Impulsiveness: Sometimes, we ADD types have a conviction, despite the total lack of data to justify it, and we simply act on that impulse. This can lead us astray or cause us to overreact, but it can also help in a crisis. Back in 1997, the UPS labor union was negotiating with management, and I had a feeling that there would be a strike, even though similar negotiations had recently taken place and been resolved. Our catalog business was totally dependent on UPS for shipping. I called a meeting of my staff and ordered everyone to stop what they were doing and come up with a plan for what we would do if UPS went on strike. One of my employees asked why we had to worry about this before the strike started. I told the employee to just do it and do it now. Within a few hours we had an account set up with FedEx and were ready to operate our shipping systems the next day. As a result of my impulse,

our company did not lose a day in shipping to our customers and stayed in operation during the UPS work stoppage. Our switch of couriers was a now-or-never move, I should point out. FedEx would not take on any new customers beginning the minute UPS announced its strike. Shades of Light was not a new customer—we had a one-day-old account.

4. Ability to get things done quickly: The ability to make quick decisions, to act on them, to underestimate the time to complete them and a high-gear drive allows ADD people to accomplish a lot in a short period of time. Others marvel at how much we get done in the time we have. They grow tired watching us. Although we can be impulsive, we have the ability to make decisions quickly and to act on them. We are not afraid to make the tough calls.

5. Ability to assimilate a lot of information and come up with a solution that anticipates trends: Because we don't intensely focus on the details and we naturally focus on the big picture, we can often see things before others, and this helps us stay ahead of the competition.

6. Closure on tasks and projects: Because we are extremely driven and like to accomplish things, we can successfully finish a project. Often people fail to see that we do actually complete things. They only see our desks and cars in great disarray and notice how many projects we have going. It's hard for them to understand that this speedy completion can be extremely valuable in running a business. When we first decided to create a website in 1995, my employees wanted

to add all the bells and whistles to it before taking it live. I looked at the site, saw merchandise on it, saw that a customer could place an order, and said, "This is great. Let's go live now, and you can enhance it later and then update the site." My employees are still enhancing our website to this day.

7. Impatience: ADD people are not patient with themselves or with anyone else. We always try to do too much in a day and lowball the amount of time projected to do the task. One important function of a manager is to give employees deadlines so that they can accomplish their tasks on time and feel good about their job and the company. One of the ways I dealt with my impatience on this subject was to discuss deadlines with my employees and get their input on what was a reasonable timeframe for the job in question. My IT/Web manager's favorite story of me is about the day I asked him to build a new website in two weeks. By the time we had finished discussing the process, we agreed it would take six months.

8. Interrupting: ADD people are notorious for interrupting others. Our brains are always in high gear and most people don't think as quickly as we do. Often, when meeting with employees, I forced myself to take notes on what I wanted to say rather than interrupting others. When they were finished talking, I would go over the five or 10 points I had thought of while they were talking. I am definitely far from perfect on this strategy.

9. Easily overwhelmed: Because we underestimate the time it takes to do something and because we try to accomplish too much, we occasionally become overwhelmed and can sometimes get upset and emotional. Relaxation and exercise can help us overcome the stress. Since we are unable to relax or sit still, a run or a gym workout is the only real solution.

## MENTAL POST-ITS FOR ADD CEOS:

1. Learn to meditate. This will be extremely hard for you since it requires completely erasing your mind of all thoughts. I focus on a "blank blackboard." Meditation is the only way to quiet our minds (without medication) so that we can fall back asleep.

2. Use Post-Its to remember appointments, things to do, things to take with you. The inside of an exit door at home, the car dashboard, and the place at work where you leave your keys are all good places for Post-Its.

3. Set aside time every day to get organized. Use technology to help you stay organized. If you lose your phone or keys, there is a gizmo you can get that beeps if your phone is separated from your keys. Smart phones and iPads really can help an ADD person. At this moment, I am writing this book on my iPad on a boat. If I had papers, I would lose them. I carry my iPad everywhere with me. Otherwise I'm sure the pages of this book would have gotten lost.

4. Keep only one to-do list and train yourself to keep it with you at all times. If you use paper, keep the pad on your desk attached in a special place or at the bottom of your computer screen. But even better is to use smartphone technology for this list. Then prioritize and use asterisks to indicate the subset of tasks that is reasonable to finish in that day. Keep your grocery list and gift ideas on your smartphone as well.

5. Set up one "mess room" with wall-to-wall shelves to hold all your projects, clutter, reading material, and other things you think you need. Find an unencumbered space elsewhere that will be for work only, not storage. Collect what you need from the mess room, bring it to the clean, bare workspace. Do your work, and then return all materials to your junk room. Don't let your spouse in this room. If your office looks like mine, train your assistant to escort all clients to your conference room, or any other comfortable area from which no one can see your desk.

6. Every time you become upset or angry about a business-related matter, write it down on your computer spreadsheet, rate it on a scale of 1 to 10, for overall importance, and then enter possible solutions. Believe it or not, this will actually help you to stay calmer and not hyperfocus on a small problem. You will quickly learn to come back the next day and recheck the list to decide whether the recent entries are important. If you decide they are, you can begin addressing them. If you become upset in a meeting, take notes about what you are feeling and why. Write down the exact words

that were said (for later reference). Hint: This is not an easy habit to form by any stretch of the imagination. But it's well worth doing.

7.  Learn to grant yourself "timeouts" when you get upset or overstimulated. Go get decaffeinated coffee from Starbucks, take a walk around the block, or simply detour into the restroom. Exercise is very important to us ADD people. It helps calm us down and gives us time to focus.

8.  Use your smartphone to set audio reminders. If you don't have a smartphone, buy one. If you don't know how to use a smartphone, have your kids or a tech-savvy friend show you.

9.  Break your annual goals into monthly goals and the monthly goals into weekly goals, all with measurable results. Review these lists every week and every month (depending on the goal). This keeps you focused on the priorities you most need.

10.  Take a pad and pencil to all meetings and lectures so that you can take notes and draw pictures to help you pay attention. I also used this for employee "chats."

11.  Don't stay in a job that does not allow some creativity. You are extremely creative and will thrive in a creative environment.

12. Decide how much time each week you would like to spend on work, family, friends, exercise, chores, e-mail, Web surfing, projects, and downtime. Record it on an excel spreadsheet and then schedule your calendar. Review every Sunday evening. Try to remember to stop once you've spent your allotted time for the week.

13. Keep a running list on your home computer or smartphone of all your nonwork projects, adding to it every time you have a whim. Try to let go of some every month.

These 13 guidelines are also available on the website as Post-Its, or you can print them and put them on Post-Its to remind you to follow them.

# Stages My Company (and I) Went Through

Although I didn't realize it at the time, my business went through stages. This became clear to me through a CEO peer group I belonged to. As we shared problems and successes, I noticed that their companies were in places mine had been. So I named the stages:

Stage 1: I can do it all myself

Stage 2: The roller-coaster

Stage 3: Shotgun approach to growth

Stage 4: The inmates are running the asylum (and I'm drowning)

Stage 5: The life ring

Stage 6: The day I became CEO

Stage 7: Milk the cow

Stage 8: The end game

Stage 9: After the sale

# STAGE 1: I CAN DO IT ALL MYSELF

**The context:** optimism and excitement reign
**Highlight:** start-up to $1,000,000 in sales
**Timeframe:** 1986–94

In the initial stage, I did it all. I answered questions, micromanaged, worked alongside every employee, knew all my employees personally, waited on customers and generally jumped in everywhere. I had no formal policies or accountability. This is an ADD paradise but can be chaotic for everyone else.

As an ADD manager, I didn't think it was necessary to know much about new areas before venturing in. When I first got interested in landscape lighting, I simply selected some merchandise and placed the order. The entrance of my husband into the business occurred after I realized that the calculations and assembly of a landscape lighting project were far too complicated for me to focus on and learn. On the other hand, he studied it and picked it right up. So we would go out at night and do customer presentations to get increased business for our small but growing retail store.

This stage is really fun for the ADD entrepreneur because bouncing around and being able to track so many things at once is enjoyable and a big asset in developing a company. You can operate successfully by the seat of your pants, at least for a while. Everyone lives in the present when you're operating this way. There is a lot of joy and discovery in it. The passion and positive outlook that ADD people have is also a major factor in success at this stage. You know employees and customers by name and changes are so easy to implement.

### Quick Test: Are you in Stage 1?

1. All employees are "managed" directly by you some of the time and you know them all by name.
2. You have time to be with customers or clients at least half the day and you know many by name.
3. Almost everything is fun and new.
4. Fewer than 10 standard formal reports are generated weekly and monthly.
5. You fill the role of more than three positions (CEO, marketing director, sales manager, buyer, etc.)
6. Your company has no formal written job descriptions, much less updated ones.
7. The emotional side is exhilarating but lonely.

## STAGE 2: THE ROLLER COASTER

**The context:** unprofitable years alternating with profitable years
**Highlight:** growth from $1,000,000 to $5,000,000 in sales
**Timeframe:** 1995–2000

I had always thought it would be a good idea to grow via mail-order catalog sales, which was a very popular business concept in the 1990s. In 1995, with no idea how much a mail-order business would cost to launch and take to profitability, I of course jumped right in. I hired a friend and graphic artist to design the catalog and an in-state printer to print it. The cost to get that first catalog produced was more than three times per copy versus what we pay today. After much searching for a consultant to help us, I telephoned a veteran cataloguer, Philip Klaus, whose kids I had taught to ski and who had built a successful children's clothing catalog, sold it, and then bought it back for pennies on the dollar. I convinced Philip to mentor me on this project. Through the years he always gave us good advice and sometimes I didn't follow it, always to find out too late that he was right. We will be forever grateful to him for his guidance. He later encouraged us to add more categories of product to our catalog.

The start-up costs of a catalog business turned out to be frightening. We set up a warehouse and stocked it with inventory worth $150,000. It cost $150,000 to produce and mail the first catalog (only 100,000 copies). We got a fancy phone system and hired personnel to cover our call center. We hired a circulation consultant to get the right lists of prospects to mail to. We gradually increased the number of catalogs mailed each year. It was costing approximately $250,000 to put a catalog drop in the mail.

Just as the catalog started breaking even, we incurred massive costs due to our growth. We had outgrown the office space above our retail store, so in 2000 we moved the retail and office operations to a larger building. It cost approximately $200,000 for improvements and the move. We succeeded in selling our previous location for the same price we had paid for our new location, meanwhile adding three times the square footage. We also moved the warehouse to a larger space and increased our inventories to keep up with our growth. This is when I lost control of the inventory, a messy situation that would prevail for several years. Discontinued catalog merchandise was building to the point at which our annual warehouse sale would not fully liquidate it. We addressed that by opening a clearance store in 2000. Yes, that entailed additional hefty setup costs and cash requirements.

I was still wearing way too many hats, trying to figure out this new business we were in, and didn't have the personnel to wear any of them for me. So in 2000 I hired an operations manager and a part-time CPA. Administrative costs doubled. Cash flow problems were massive and expenses caused a loss in 2000 and 2001. I stopped taking a salary.

## Timeline of major events during these years:

1995  Launched mail-order catalog and hired coach;

1995  Set up and later moved warehouse to accommodate catalog merchandise;

1996  Hired circulation consultant for catalog ($60,000 a year);

1999  Hired outsource CPA on a part-time basis since we couldn't afford one in-house;

2000  Moved main store to 15,000-square-foot building (which we bought personally);

2000  Set up outlet store;

2000  Hired operations manager.

## Quick Test: Are you in Stage 2 now?

1. Difficulty processing paperwork, getting receipts, and obtaining accurate reports;

2. You are so busy working *in* the business, there is literally no time to work *on* the business;

3. Revenues show double-digit increases;

4. The bottom line seesaws up and down;

5. No matter how hard you work, profits are not great.

## STAGE 3: SHOTGUN APPROACH TO GROWTH

**The context:** organizational breakdown and lack of strategic direction
**Highlight:** sales grow from $5 million to $12 million
**Timeframe:** 2001–5

ADD types thrive in conditions of dynamic change and growth, but even we have our limits in that regard. When I think back to the early 2000s, I have pictures of the staff running in circles and our operation resembling a rudderless ship. But we were growing, and that covers a lot of sins. We doubled the number of catalogs we were mailing annually. Catalog sales more than doubled during this period. Our main retail store sales increased by 50 percent in the new location. In spite of ourselves, we had wonderfully profitable years from 2002 to 2005. Yet cash requirements for growth in personnel—up to 50 employees from 20—and goods to sell—a standing inventory up to $2 million at wholesale—were strangling us.

We hired a full-time IT manager and an accounting manager (who was not a CPA). Our administrative costs tripled during these years. We set up our website in 2000 while adding rugs, curtains, some accent furniture, and other accessories to our product mix in the catalog. That of course meant more pages to print and mail, which raised catalog overhead. We closed our outlet store across the street from the main retail store and found a new location on the other side of town on a sublease. The new store set-up brought more cash requirements.

We promoted our former outlet store manager to call center manager in 2002. She recalls this time by repeating what a coworker said to her offhandedly one day: "The coworker said I must be spending too much time with Ashton, and that ADD might be contagious, because during a two-minute conversation I had just changed topics five times." In 2003 we let our circulation consultant go and brought that function in-house. We hired a new manager when we reopened the outlet store in 2003. We let our operations manager go because we didn't feel this position was worth the cost, so I was once again managing everyone. We lost our main store manager in 2005. Unfortunately, I desperately hired a few crazy people to fill all these vacancies. My distribution manager recently looked back on this time and summed it up as follows: "Meetings within meetings and sometimes even meetings within meetings within meetings. There should have been a revolving door on your office," he told me, adding, "I didn't always appreciate the continuous interruptions during our meetings, but I always appreciated the fact that you never told someone you didn't have time to hear their concerns." Bad times lay ahead.

*Use your smartphone to set audio reminders. If you don't have a smartphone, buy one. If you don't know how to use a smartphone, have your kids or a tech-savvy friend show you.*

## Timeline of major events during these years:

2000    Started www.ShadesOfLight.com;

2002    Moved warehouse again (to 30,000 square feet);

2002    Moved outlet store (closed for 10 months during that time);

2002    Losses turn into profits;

2003    Added rugs to lighting catalog;

2003    Changed circulation consultants to save money;

2004 Added curtains to catalog;

2004 All-time-high circulation of 3,900,000 catalogs;

2004 Administrative costs increased 24 percent;

2005 Sales dropped 13 percent;

2005 Let operations manager go.

### Quick Test: Are you in Stage 3 now?

1. You begin setting up job descriptions and attempt to conduct employee reviews.
2. Your managers are running everything by you before they act.
3. Revenues continue to increase but average closer to 10 percent a year.
4. Your costs are increasing faster than your revenues.
5. You see reasonable profits, though unimpressive cash flow.

## STAGE 4: THE INMATES ARE RUNNING THE ASYLUM

**The context:** revenues weakening, problems multiplying

**Highlight:** recruitment of a true CFO

**Timeframe:** 2006

Sometime in 2006 our profits turned into losses. Unfortunately my focus wasn't on our income statement; it was on putting out the fires caused by the passive–aggressive people I had been hiring (see Chapter 5 for more on this personality). Employees and managers spent all day talking behind peoples' backs and complaining about everything they could think of. Drama queens all over the company spent their day finding things other people were doing wrong and creating or magnifying problems. Customer service levels fell in both the retail sector and

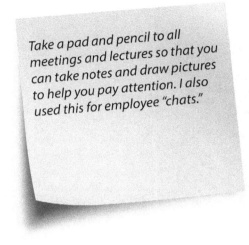

*Take a pad and pencil to all meetings and lectures so that you can take notes and draw pictures to help you pay attention. I also used this for employee "chats."*

the catalog division. The employees did not work well as a team.

As sales fell, we desperately hired back our outside circulation consultant, thinking that would fix the problem. He simply encouraged us to mail more catalogs, which in turn increased our loss.

On top of all this, Home Depot started mailing a high-end catalog, 10 Crescent Lane, to our customers in late 2005. The effort didn't succeed and was discontinued a year later, but in the meantime it put a drag on our mail-order sales. I had a series of weak merchandise buyers selecting product for the catalog, and I had no time to oversee or analyze the situation.

And on top of it all, I decided to open a new retail store in Virginia Beach to test the concept of retail store expansion. In hindsight, this was not a great choice during a time of losses and cash flow drains, but I was desperately trying to find a way to ensure future growth since I saw the Internet as a source of increasing competition.

Our administrative costs were at an all-time high. We were overstaffed in some places, but this was not obvious because people ran around gossiping all day instead of working. In September 2006 I hired a real CFO. I actually spent three months of intense searching and interviewing to make sure I got the right person this time. If she had known what she was getting into, she would never have taken the job. I was putting out fires all day instead of managing. I had completely lost control of my company.

*Learn to grant yourself "timeouts" when you get upset or overstimulated. Go get decaffeinated coffee from Starbucks, take a walk around the block, or simply detour into the restroom. Exercise is very important to us ADD people. It helps calm us down and gives us time to focus.*

**Symptoms of turmoil (how I knew I had lost control of the business):**

- My husband arrived at the warehouse to find the staff smoking pot on the loading dock.
- I caught an employee embezzling funds.
- Employee theft was an issue and inaccurate inventory records were rampant.
- Inventory levels had spiraled out of control.
- Financial statements were unreliable and very tardy, and even I could find faults in them.
- Customer service complaints were frequent.
- Employees refused to do things I asked or completely ignored requests, knowing full well I was too busy putting out fires to follow up.
- At the end of my day, I hadn't gotten to one thing on my to-do list, much less met with a single manager to set goals or obtain progress reports.

Every time you become upset or angry about a business-related matter, write it down on a computer spreadsheet, rate it on a scale of 1 to 10 for overall importance, and then enter possible solutions. Believe it or not, this will actually help you to stay calmer and not hyperfocus on a small problem. Then come back the next day and decide which issues to address.

If you become upset in a meeting, take notes about what you are feeling and why. Write down the exact words that were said (for later reference). Hint: This is not an easy habit to form by any stretch of the imagination. But it's well worth doing.

## Quick test: Are you in Stage 4 now?

1. You spend 50 percent or more of your time with employee issues or making quick fixes to problems, both internal and external.
2. At least one employee in three is complaining about something, someone, what you are making them do, what isn't going right in the company, and your decision making.
3. Your managers are making their own decisions, often contrary to your wishes.
4. Revenues decrease, likely for the first time.
5. You are losing customers.
6. Your bottom line is decreasing.
7. You have a bad feeling about your employees, the business, the future.
8. Work is no longer fun. In fact, you dread going in.
9. Work issues keep you awake at night (more than normal).

10. You have more reports than you have time to look at.
11. You have difficulty in getting paperwork, receipts, and reports from key departments.
12. Reports you do get are often inaccurate.
13. Client issues are frequent and customer complaints increase.
14. Cash flow isn't what it needs to be.
15. You get constant calls from the office on your cell phone when you are not at work.

## STAGE 5: THE LIFE RING

**The context:** help from outside is needed—and arrives
**Highlight:** new strategy mapped by our consultant
**Timeframe:** 2007–8

In 2007 I realized I desperately needed to make changes but didn't have much confidence in my ability to make them. Thankfully my ADD came to the rescue and I started thinking strategically. We bought a warehouse in an enterprise zone, resulting in a savings of $60,000 a year in costs, even with the mortgage payments that came with 100 percent financing. I realized that we might be overmailing catalogs (our marketing costs for the mailings were up to 25 percent of sales), and I started doing my own circulation plan, cutting the numbers back. We went from 3,900,000 to 3,470,000 catalogs mailed annually and later dropped that to 1,900,000). Then I started looking for strategic help.

I had tried to find a sounding board through a CEO peer group, but that didn't work because my business was a stage ahead of theirs and also larger, so our problems were different. Then I tried a board of directors composed of successful friends and entrepreneurs, but that didn't work either, since they were taking the view from 30,000 feet, so to speak, and I needed someone at 10,000 feet. Finally, a fellow ADD/CEO friend recommended a strategic consultant, Steve Kimball, whom he had been impressed with at a conference. Being desperate, I immediately arranged to meet with Steve. Although it cost us $120,000 over a 30-month period, this was the life ring I needed to turn the business into a profit machine.

Our consultant had a nonthreatening manner, which right away contributed to his effectiveness. He helped me take a step back and look at my business from a new perspective. He helped me devise a crisis plan (see my Yellow-Orange-Red 3-level Crisis Management Plan in Chapter 5). Then he helped me devise status boards that would allow my managers and me to monitor our operation's top-priority issues. In my case it was sales by division, costs in general (i.e., catalog production, administration, warehouse expenses), costs as a percentage of sales, profits by division, inventory levels, and back-order levels (see Dashboards in Chapter 4).

Steve recommended some addition-by-subtraction measures, most notably in our product offerings. One suggested cut was curtains, which represented 16 percent of our sales, so you can imagine my misgivings, at a point when sales and profits were down. Other categories he suggested we eliminate were custom-order items (too distracting for a company our size), accessories, and any category that did not reach $50,000 in annual sales. In order to walk away from the sales volume these categories had been providing, we would have to cut costs.

Around that time, the stock market crashed (September–October 2008) so I had to implement the first stage of my crisis plan (see Code Yellow in Chapter 5), which included layoffs of 20 percent. I met with managers from each department and asked each one for a downsizing plan. Most decided to lay off their least productive employee. In the warehouse, all employees went on a 30-hour work week with appropriate pay cuts. So we went through a series of meetings with employees to lay them off. This was the most painful thing I've ever had to do. It was excruciating to have to put people on the street when economic times were bad and they were sure to have trouble getting work. An offer was made to help them with resume writing and job seeking, although only some took advantage. As we cut the additional expenses listed on my crisis plan, our vital signs started to improve. By the end of 2008 we had turned the corner.

My friend Jay Cowan, CEO of River Cross Partners, a business strategy firm specializing in succession planning, called it his Offense and Defense Strategy. Jay says, "It can be hard not to do things that are 'easy' but not important, just to feel you are accomplishing something. We defined this as *offense* and *defense*. *Offense* consisted of activities relating to increasing revenues, while *defense* was made up of tasks that were something else." The something else in our situation was decreasing costs and holding all employees accountable.

> Break your annual goals into monthly goals and the monthly goals into weekly goals, all with measurable results. Review these lists every week and every month (depending on the goal). This keeps you focused on the priorities you most need.

## Quick Test: Are you in Stage 5 now?

1. You question your decision making and your capacity to lead.

2. Cash flow remains a problem.

3. You find a coach or partner who sees the big picture and is not critical of your style.

4. You start to analyze what is actually making you money—in other words, worthy of your time and energy.

5. You let go of nonproductive revenue streams.

6. You bring your business down to a revenue level that restores a sense of control.

7. You start to design new reports and set up your own dashboard.

8. You make and carry out decisions to get your costs back in control.

9. You set up a weekly meeting with everyone who directly reports to you (although you are not at the point where you can actually make the meetings happen every week).

10. You set up incentive bonuses for positions that previously did not have them.

11. You feel the first signs of hope.

## STAGE 6: THE DAY I BECAME CEO

**The context:** reality-based management, focused on fewer goals
**Highlight:** Shades of Light returns to profitability
**Timeframe:** 2009

Our consultant, Steve, my husband, Dave, my CFO, and I met on a regular basis to review progress and keep me pointed in the right direction so I would no longer let distractions eat up all my time. I got better at controlling my workday and focused more on the highest priorities (see How to Set Up Dashboards in Chapter 4). As the stock market went down and the U.S. economy continued to weaken, I had to implement the next stage of my Crisis Plan (see Code Orange in Chapter 5). I reduced our catalog mailings 50 percent and thus had to further reduce expenses. That took us to my next level of crisis management (see Code Red in Chapter 5).

Steve helped us decide on two—and only two—goals for growth. The goals we chose were to double online sales volume and double contract sales. By this time the cut in catalog circulation had caused revenue to drop to $8.6 million versus $12.5 million four years earlier.

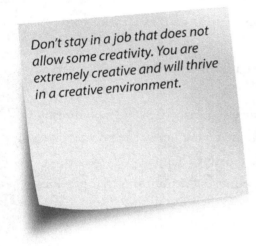

*Don't stay in a job that does not allow some creativity. You are extremely creative and will thrive in a creative environment.*

My days were filled with meetings and managing (see Chapter 4 for my Weekly Meeting Checklist and call center weekly report). I had always run monthly managers' meetings at which each manager would share his or her most important accomplishment of the previous month, and then I or an outside specialist would train the managers in one area, be it time management, reporting practices, or something else. I was constantly requiring my managers to do employee write-ups or Clarification of Job Expectations, as we called them (see Chapter 5 for these forms). I strictly enforced our First-Call Resolution policy (see Chapter 5). Our consultant, Steve, helped me set up bonus plans for employees so, as sales climbed, employees got extra compensation. These weren't straight salary bumps, which meant I was covered in case sales ever fell again. We also started doing monthly contests to encourage and reinforce sales personnel (see Bonuses and Sales Contests in Chapter 5). I set up a weekly brainstorming Web meeting with our Web guru, his manager, the marketing manager, and myself with the goal of doubling Web sales. I gave us all weekly "homework," and then we reviewed the results at the next week's meeting. I hired a contract sales manager and set her up with a bid-reporting spreadsheet that we reviewed biweekly. Gradually both Web sales and contract sales started to grow.

I created a job description for myself as CEO (see Chapter 5) and then proceeded to follow the list of the tasks. I spent time doing the things I was responsible for doing, not the things I wanted to do. My CFO set up inventory meetings, and I established goals for every division and every category of product based on sales. The levels were so far off from goal that we had to set attainable interim targets. By the middle of 2009, cash flow was much improved. Meanwhile, inventory was under control and our losses had turned into profits. For the first time in our history, we paid suppliers early.

### How creating and following a CEO job description made me more effective:

1. I spent time analyzing the important numbers—sales, costs, gross margin—and I found problems. I drilled down to learn more. It's really that simple.
2. I held people accountable. This required weekly, biweekly, or monthly meetings to review the metrics of the business with each department head.
3. I negotiated reductions starting with the largest costs and working down.

4. I set up incentive bonus plans for key employees. Since their salaries had been reduced, I simply used bonus plans (see Chapter 5) instead of raises.

5. I celebrated successes. At my monthly managers' meeting, I had each person share their greatest success from the previous month. I set up a bulletin board where we posted good things employees had done. I created a recognition form for managers to bring to the monthly meeting for people they wanted to recognize, and these forms went on a company bulletin board, visible to all.

6. I focused my efforts on revenue generators. We ramped up our e-mail marketing to consumers, increased online advertising (blog ads), started a social-media marketing campaign (Facebook, Pinterest, etc.), set up a booth at hotel trade shows, and revamped the main page of our website to boost sales volume.

## Quick Test: Are you in Stage 6 now? (Translation: have you finally become your CEO?)

1. You no longer tolerate low producers, passive–aggressive behavior, or procrastinators. You finally spend your time addressing these matters instead of putting out fires.

2. Most of your day is spent analyzing reports, setting goals, and following up on goals already set with your managers.

3. You have designed reports that only show you what you really need to monitor.

4. You have set two main goals for the year and put items on your to-do list that relate to those two goals.

5. You have time to brainstorm and analyze steps toward achieving those two goals.

6. Your office is no longer is a revolving door.
7. If a staff member calls your cell phone, it is a true emergency.
8. You are comfortably paying off your debts.
9. You are finally able to give yourself a raise.
10. You no longer dread coming to work.

## STAGE 7: MILK THE COW

**The context:** operational efficiency trumps a weak economy
**Highlight:** sales climb back up to $12.6 million with healthy cash flow
**Timeframe:** 2010–11

Back on track, with capable managers helping me achieve the company's goals, this became a sweet spot for the business I had launched some 20 years earlier. Sales climbed and profits consistently outperformed the industry—all this while the U.S. economy drifted weakly along. During these challenging economic years, our net profits were greater than 10 percent. Our customer surveys were coming back with glowing accolades—a most welcome change. The new Virginia Beach store, with its third manager, finally started making money. Main store profits were up 44 percent. Our outlet store also turned a profit in 2011, which was a first. Catalog division profits increased by 5.5 times from 2007 to 2011. Administrative overhead remained down 18 percent from its high in 2007. Sales climbed back to $12,665,000 in 2011. Finally, a cash cow.

I decided that every week, I needed to make one move to increase revenues and one move to decrease costs. I spent many hours analyzing results to come up with ideas for our Offense and Defense strategy. This forced me to look at the big picture to see where I could make the most impact. My dashboards brought to my attention a few obvious issues:

1. We were spending too high a percentage of sales to produce and mail the catalog. Seeing this, I ordered a cut in circulation.

2. If I could make a small dent in our largest single expense, it would result in a positive cumulative effect on the bottom line. So I joined a committee to meet with the United States Postal Service, our single largest vendor, dollarwise. Then I negotiated FedEx versus UPS to yield a significant cost savings. From the trash pick-up to outside consultants, I managed to lower cost after cost.

3. I even renegotiated all our rents. You would be surprised what discounts you can get when times are bad.

4. We refinanced the mortgage on our office/retail building, thereby saving $70,000 a year.

5. I contacted my largest vendors and negotiated special discounts.

It all added up to an enormous bottom-line improvement. My weekly chores included the following:

1. Studying the lowest-performing sales sectors (such as catalog table lamps) and setting up brainstorming sessions with buyers, marketing, etc., to change our strategy;

2. Swapping out our existing checking account to one that paid interest, a logical move, since we finally were producing positive cash flow;

3. Setting up dashboards to measure productivity across the company;

4. Ordering energy-saving bulbs (yes, we had to make this a goal and we're a lighting store) for all store displays;

5. Reviewing our competitive advantages and researching online to see what discounters might be doing to us. At that point I decided that an additional goal would be to increase our percentage of exclusive products, on which we made a full margin. That would balance the discounting we were having to do to compete on the Internet.

6. Setting up quarterly meetings for all merchandise buyers to talk about trends and plan goals for each buying market;

7. Generally paying a lot of attention to marketing efforts, to the point that I hired a dedicated marketing and sales manager. I set up quarterly marketing meetings where we brainstormed with buyers, creative and marketing personnel to sketch out all promotions, website features, social marketing efforts, blog advertising and blog articles. Weekly and quarterly, we analyzed what was working and what wasn't in our marketing efforts.

8. Analyzing our e-commerce results and looking to lift them led to ideas such as an online "outlet sale."

Although this was a lot of work and required an inordinate amount of focus, especially for an ADD person, these efforts were very rewarding financially. Being ADD, I didn't know how long I could keep it up, and since my husband was 66 years old, we made the decision to sell the company. We had missed one high point in our profitability, and I didn't want to miss another one.

## STAGE 8: THE END GAME

**Context:** selling our "baby"
**Highlight:** closing the deal
**Timeframe:** 2011

Early in the history of Shades of Light, we prepaid a company $25,000 to create a prospectus that supposedly was going to get us sold. No such thing happened at the time. It led me to a rule of thumb: don't prepay a broker to sell your company. This time around, we used our strategic consultant to help us lay out a plan. He and I contacted brokers who would present proposals on how best to sell the business. Many of those we contacted said we were too small for them to take on. In the process, one broker said, "I think I have a fit. If you want to pursue it, we will introduce you, and if it works, you will owe us a commission, and if it doesn't, you owe us nothing." That set us in motion. The discussions proceeded smoothly, and we really liked the two managers whom the purchasers planned to bring in to run the business for them. Unexpectedly, however, those two managers had to back out. That left us suddenly dealing with "sharp shooters" about whom we had a bad feeling. We were concerned that all our employees would be allowed to remain employed, and we were ready to back out when, all of a sudden, in came an offer from the broker himself. We really liked this guy and his partner and knew it would be a great fit. Meanwhile we contacted one of the other brokers to see if he could find a higher bid than the one we had. The deal was if he could beat the offer, we would owe him a commission on the increase, even if we didn't take that offer. Unfortunately, because most companies were just coming out of the recession, no one was buying retail companies except for distress sales. But we felt that we were getting a fair price, and we wanted to sell and retire.

So I worked 24/7 preparing documents for the due diligence. After several months of no sleep, we reached a point where I was fairly sure the financing was solid and the sale would go through. I brought in my CFO to help me. Between my CFO, my accountant, my attorney, my husband manning the copy machine, and sleepless nights, we arrived at our closing four months after the offer was accepted.

For the day when you're ready to sell your business, here are some recommendations.

## The sales package:

1. If you own your buildings—hopefully you do by now—negotiate long-term leases. (I strongly recommend you own your buildings, even while you are growing).
2. Negotiate cash at closing, as much as you can get.
3. Negotiate a percentage of sales (not profits since you can no longer control pricing or costs) as an earn-out.
4. Negotiate your compensation such that your CEO pay level and benefits stay the same, but you are only working 30 hours a week. No one knows your business better than you (not even if the new owners are in the same business), and you can still bring in sales better than anyone else.
5. If you have any special skills such as product or process design, negotiate royalties if you can.
6. Decide what is important to you: money or your people. If it's your personnel, be sure to sell to people you feel comfortable with, who will take care of your employees, even if it may mean less money.

## STAGE 9: AFTER THE SALE

**The context:** striving to be one big, happy family
**Highlight:** if you continue to work under new ownership at the company, negotiate to only do what you love.
**Timeframe:** 2012

After the sale closed, I spent the first six months teaching the new owners the business. They were new to our industry but proved to be extremely quick learners. Since they were used to working with higher-level managers, the first important lesson I taught them was to never believe employees—you've got to double-check all reports and data.

Sales soared. Business climbed by 20 percent from the day they took over, continuing the steady upward trajectory we had it on. After the first six months, the new owners were really running the business, and I was struggling to learn my new job and adjust to being an employee. This was very tough since I always had an opinion and was used to being in charge. But I had to let them find their way while I focused on the areas they had hired me to help with. It took me the entire second six months to figure out how to do my job well. I even wrote my own job description, listing annual goals and measuring them monthly (see my after-the-sale job description in Chapter 5). In that time period I designed the company's number-one new product: a bushel basket lantern. My biggest challenge was that since sales were up, the staff was so overworked they couldn't get my product designs made, photographed, or set up in the computer. I addressed this with the new owners. My message was that the Internet was really starting to hurt us with discounting and free shipping, such that we needed to increase our volume of exclusive products. Doing so meant dealing with higher margins and making a much stronger impression on the consumer. So they created new positions and hired personnel. It took the full second six months to get this going and for me to figure out a smooth process to make it all work. At last I could simply do "the fun stuff," not have to manage people, and have my weekends off.

Keep a running list on your home computer or smartphone of all your nonwork projects, adding to it every time you have a whim. Try to finish one (or let go of one) BEFORE adding each new one!

## What I have learned from the new owners:

1. They are more laid-back than I am. Thus they are more patient, more analytical, and better managers and strategic thinkers.
2. They don't get caught in the minutiae, so they focus on company direction better.
3. If you leave people alone and let them do their job, the results sometimes happen more smoothly.
4. They have a philosophy: never lose money. In hindsight I have wondered what it would have been like if I had shared that rule. I might not have made so many decisions that led me to lose money. I also would have reacted much more quickly when things started going south. So, you live and learn.

# Chapter 4

# KISS Management

There are five simple steps to managing people. First you write a compelling classified advertisement to attract the people you want to respond. Then you ask them tricky questions before you let them know what you are looking for. Be careful not to hire someone simply because you like him or her. Always focus on former accomplishments, making sure to check out references. Never ask leading questions that clue in the candidate to what you are looking for. Never promise anything in an interview (or, for that matter, in an employee review).

After you hire the candidate, make sure his or her training program matches the line items on the job description, that it is on a calendar, and that each person responsible for the training segment is indicated on the calendar. Then distribute the calendars and follow up weekly.

Always be clear and provide written job expectations. This takes some time to lay out, so budget that time. Establish tolerance levels. Communicate all this in writing and have the new hire sign it for the personnel file. Use this for write-ups (see below) and annual reviews. Once the goals and expectations are clear, you must have regular meetings and record (write-up) whenever expectations aren't met.

# MANAGEMENT MADE SIMPLE: FIVE STEPS

## 1. Recruiting

Writing an effective advertisement for personnel takes practice and thought. Keep in mind the purpose of the advertisement and whom you want to attract. You want your job opening to sound better to the right person than all other similar classified advertisements. Remember, the goal of the advertisement is to get the best people in the door. You can cover the negatives in the interview (occasional weekend work, etc.). You need to decide prior to interviewing whether "experience" or "qualities" are more important. I believe you can train people, but you can't give them superior creativity, intelligence, analytical ability, or any of those assets.

a. Think of a clever title for the position.
   i. Boredom-free receptionist work
   ii. The trendiest new restaurant is looking for...
   iii. Award-winning builder needs...

b. Explain the most important benefits you have to offer candidates.
   i. First, list all the benefits and advantages of working for your company. Hopefully this is not a list of employee benefits. Then select one or two that would make the right person eager to apply for this job.
   ii. "Flexible hours make this the perfect job for a student or mother."
   iii. "Flexible vacation schedule allows travel-lovers the freedom they are looking for."

c. Start out with an active word and a catchy statement.
   i. "Play an important role in someone's most special day by helping them select their wedding wardrobe and accessories."
   ii. "Meet all the beautiful people working in our upscale…"
   iii. "Get paid to learn the secrets of French cooking…"

d. Explain what the job actually entails.
   i. Often the advertisement does not give clues as to what the job is all about.
   ii. Be clear. Don't use industry words that potential candidates might not know.

e. Use positive language and phrases.
   i. "Drug-testing" (negative) vs. "drug-free environment" (positive)
   ii. "Two Saturdays a month required" vs. "only two Saturdays a month"

f. Use strong words.
   i. "High-end" retail store…(weak) vs. "the premier…" (stronger)
   ii. "Benefits included" vs. "competitive benefits package."

g. Make it sound exciting and fun.

h. Don't make it sound too good to be true ("Top compensation and benefits").

i. Don't reveal the characteristics you are looking for. Only mention the skills necessary.

    i. Don't be too vague ("Join a great restaurant team").

    ii. Make sure you clearly indicate necessary skills (impeccable driving record, adept at using small tools, analytically inclined, etc.).

    iii. Don't tell candidates you are looking for a self-starter, high accuracy, organizational skills, communication skills, etc. (Find these out in the interview.)

j. Never misspell.

k. Explain what the job is and what the business is about (unless it is very well known or you're creating a "blind" advertisement).

l. Check candidates out on Facebook, LinkedIn, MySpace, etc., before you bring them in for an interview. Then get them to come to your office to fill out an application so you can prescreen them before spending time interviewing. We recruited most of our staff through Craigslist, LinkedIn, and Facebook. With the Internet, researching employees before interviewing is simple.

**Example of a poorly written "want ad":**

The _____ Hotel and Spa, a _____ Property, is currently seeking an Accounting Manager. Ideal candidate should be a hard-working individual with experience in the hotel industry (preferred but not required) and a positive attitude and commitment to customer service. This job involves AR billing, cash and credit card reconciliation. The Accounting Manager assists with payroll, month end closing, and all other aspects of accounting. This position may require work during some weekends. Working hours are predominantly Monday through Friday 8 a.m. to 5 p.m.

Simply a great place to work.

**Better:**

Bookkeeping with Benefits at a Premium Spa

Use your bookkeeping skills in a job with flexible hours and fun people. The award-winning _____ Hotel and Spa needs you for accounting responsibilities including AR billing, cash and credit card reconciliations, payroll, and month end closing. Discounted spa facilities available to employees. Competitive benefits package.

**Ineffective ad:**

International health and wellness company is currently seeking persons with a passion for helping others change their health through good, balanced nutrition. If you are seriously interested in helping others through health and wellness, respond to this post with a valid contact number to be contacted with more information. Part-time or full-time positions available. No prior experience required; training provided.

**Better:**

Do you love working out, eating healthy, and helping people? Stay in shape while getting paid. Join our energetic team at our renowned health and wellness company. Part-time and full-time positions available for this fun opportunity.

73

## 2. Interviewing

Before the interview: List the strengths needed for the position and devise questions that will reveal applicants' strengths and weaknesses. Review their resumes. Look for gaps in employment, longevity in jobs, accomplishments. See if they list courses taken, awards received, and the like.

a. Put them at ease. Find a common bond. Get them talking about themselves.

b. Never tell them about the job or the skills you are looking for before you finish interviewing them.

c. Ask them only tough, open-ended questions (not questions with yes or no answers).

d. Words to watch for (don't hire anyone who uses these):
   i. *We* did…
   ii. *You* (or *you should* instead of *I*…)
   iii. Followers (I/we *worked* on…) instead of doers (*I accomplished/did*…)
   iv. Passive (I *compiled*…) instead of active (I *researched, analyzed, and summarized*…)

e. Do not hire someone because you like him or her. Do not hire someone who gives you all the right answers in the interview. Only hire based on a record of achievement (hire "doers").

f.  Discover candidates' skills and talents. Figure out if they match the skills necessary to do the job.

g.  Look for nonverbal clues (see "are they lying?" in Chapter 5).

h.  Make sure you ask probing, not leading, questions. Examples:
    i.   Probing: What is your favorite thing to do in your free time?
    ii.  Leading: Are you good at working with your hands?

i.  Dig for the negatives. Find out why candidates left each job and probe there. Find out which boss they liked the least and probe. Ask what bugs them most about coworkers (this usually exposes their own weakness).

j.  Are they interested in us and why? What research (if any) did they do on the company or are they just interested in benefits and money?

k.  Learn to keep your mouth shut and let the candidate talk. Learn to tolerate the silence until candidates give you an answer.

l.  Always ask for the number of work days candidates missed in the last year (a great predictor of performance).

m.  Try these questions:
    i.   How did you...? (not Did you...?)
    ii.  Why did you...? (leave that job, hate that manager, like that job, try that company, make that move, etc.)

      iii.  Best-and-worst questions (covering aspects of past job, manager, experience)

      iv.  What about _____ makes it the best (worst)?

      v.  Can you tell me about…?

      vi.  Can you expound on that situation…?

      vii.  How did that affect…?

      viii. What would you like to change (if you could) about…? (your life, current job, the city, your skills, etc.)

n.  Describe yourself in three words.

o.  Tell me the difference between _____ and _____. Examples: working for Company A and Company B. Tell me the difference between analyzing the reports and summarizing them.

## 3.  Training

I always required my managers to do "training calendars" for new employees, covering all parts of the job description. I found that this was the only way they would really train new hires. I would follow up twice during the training period, once halfway through and once at the end.

## 4.  Managing

a.  Do you know what specific results you expect from each employee?

b.  Are they measurable?

c.  Does the employee know these expectations? Have they been communicated in writing?

d.  Have you followed up with checklists on a regular basis? What are the impediments that keep them from meeting expectations?

e.  When they don't meet expectations, did you discuss and document? Do you follow up via e-mail, to put things on a written record?

f.  Do you constantly challenge your managers to move out of their comfort zone?

## 5.  Recording Job Failures (the dreaded "write-up")

I was forever getting on my managers about not recording incidents, failures of service, and screw-ups on the part of their personnel. Nothing is more effective in getting the expectation across than this. In Chapter 5 I have included a copy of the various forms we used to recognize and to correct the behavior of employees. And don't forget to recognize successes (see recognition form). I had a public bulletin board at the entrance to the corporate office on which I posted these positive reports, along with the employee's picture (usually a funny one from the company party or birthday).

Don't delay in getting rid of all negative people or anyone who causes you too much stress. Likewise, dismiss any employees who take up too much of your time after initial training. No exceptions.

Dashboards: Use dashboards to see the big picture in your company. This is the most important thing you can have as CEO. Every goal you set needs a specific measure for success (usually numbers or an indicator of all-complete) and a form (spreadsheet) to track the progress.

## HOW TO SET UP DASHBOARDS

1. Decide on the most important numbers you need to monitor to keep your business on track: revenue (orders taken and orders delivered by division), cost of goods percentage, return percentages, back-orders, cancellations, inventory level, inventory turns, number of customers, number of orders, average order, accounts receivable level, accounts payable number of days, payroll costs, major cost categories (each cost center total costs, freight costs, individual costs >5 percent of total revenue, etc.).

2. Decide which costs need to be monitored weekly (sales, returns, customer service questionnaires, payroll, etc.) and which only need to be monitored monthly (distribution center, employee attrition, A/P, A/R, inventory, etc.). I kept my monthly dashboard as a year-to-date against each previous year (see below).

3. Set up comparisons to the previous year and keep in monthly/weekly format.

**My CEO Dashboard**

| Year > | 2010 | % change | 2009 | % | 2008 | % | 2007 | % | 2006 | % | 2005 | % |
|---|---|---|---|---|---|---|---|---|---|---|---|---|
| **$$$ (000)** | | | | | | | | | | | | |
| **Income** | | | | | | | | | | | | |
| Broad St. Store | | | | | | | | | | | | |
| Va Beach Store | | | | | | | | | | | | |
| Outlet Store | | | | | | | | | | | | |
| Catalog: Lighting | | | | | | | | | | | | |
| Rugs | | | | | | | | | | | | |
| Curtains | | | | | | | | | | | | |
| freight income | | | | | | | | | | | | |
| Contract | | | | | | | | | | | | |
| Total | | | | | | | | | | | | |
| **Cost of Goods Sold** | | | | | | | | | | | | |
| Broad St. Store | | | | | | | | | | | | |
| Va Beach Store | | | | | | | | | | | | |
| Outlet Store | | | | | | | | | | | | |
| Catalog: Ltg | | | | | | | | | | | | |
| Rugs | | | | | | | | | | | | |
| Curtains | | | | | | | | | | | | |
| Total | | | | | | | | | | | | |
| **Measured Costs** | | | | | | | | | | | | |
| Call Center | | | | | | | | | | | | |

continued...

| | | | | | | | | | | | | | | | | | | | | |
|---|---|---|---|---|---|---|---|---|---|---|---|---|---|---|---|---|---|---|---|---|
| Warehouse | | | | | | | | | | | | | | | | | | | | |
| Cat production | | | | | | | | | | | | | | | | | | | | |
| merchandising | | | | | | | | | | | | | | | | | | | | |
| freight in | | | | | | | | | | | | | | | | | | | | |
| freight out | | | | | | | | | | | | | | | | | | | | |
| other catalog/web costs | | | | | | | | | | | | | | | | | | | | |
| List rental income (+) | | | | | | | | | | | | | | | | | | | | |
| Damaged claims | | | | | | | | | | | | | | | | | | | | |
| Contract costs | | | | | | | | | | | | | | | | | | | | |
| **Profit (loss)** | | | | | | | | | | | | | | | | | | | | |
| Broad St Store | | | | | | | | | | | | | | | | | | | | |
| Va Beach Store | | | | | | | | | | | | | | | | | | | | |
| Outlet Store | | | | | | | | | | | | | | | | | | | | |
| Contract | | | | | | | | | | | | | | | | | | | | |
| Catalog | | | | | | | | | | | | | | | | | | | | |
| Admin O/H | | | | | | | | | | | | | | | | | | | | |
| **Total** | | | | | | | | | | | | | | | | | | | | |
| # catalogs mailed YTD | | | | | | | | | | | | | | | | | | | | |
| Delivered sales per cat | | | | | | | | | | | | | | | | | | | | |
| A/R Level | | | | | | | | | | | | | | | | | | | | |
| total inventory $ | | | | | | | | | | | | | | | | | | | | |
| Web sales | | | | | | | | | | | | | | | | | | | | |
| # Full time employees | | | | | | | | | | | | | | | | | | | | |

**My CURRENT Dashboard**

| 2012 Goals Progress | 2011 ave month | 2012 Monthly Goal | 2012 ave month | Jan | Feb | Mar | Apr | May | Jun | Jul | Aug | Sep | Oct | Nov | Dec |
|---|---|---|---|---|---|---|---|---|---|---|---|---|---|---|---|
| Product Development Progress | | | | | | | | | | | | | | | |
| total # exclusive products | | | | | | | | | | | | | | | |
| Exclusive sales (Delivered) | | | | | | | | | | | | | | | |
| % sales | | | | | | | | | | | | | | | |
| Catalog gross margin $$$ | | | | | | | | | | | | | | | |
| Catalog gross margin % | | | | | | | | | | | | | | | |
| New product category sales | | | | | | | | | | | | | | | |
| unique accent furniture | | | | | | | | | | | | | | | |
| wall clocks and wall decor | | | | | | | | | | | | | | | |
| Referring sites: | | | | | | | | | | | | | | | |
| Pinterest | | | | | | | | | | | | | | | |
| Houzz | | | | | | | | | | | | | | | |
| Olioboard | | | | | | | | | | | | | | | |
| Facebook | | | | | | | | | | | | | | | |
| Other | | | | | | | | | | | | | | | |
| Stumble Upon? | | | | | | | | | | | | | | | |
| Wanelo? | | | | | | | | | | | | | | | |

**Call Center Weekly Meeting**

| Product Development Progress | week 1 | week 2 | week 3 | week 4 | week 5 | week 6 | week 7 | week 8 | week 9 | week 10 | week 11 | week 12 | week 13 | week 14 |
|---|---|---|---|---|---|---|---|---|---|---|---|---|---|---|
| Report on the status of the following: | | | | | | | | | | | | | | |
| Personnel Schedule | | | | | | | | | | | | | | |
| Swatches (fabric & rug) | | | | | | | | | | | | | | |
| #"Do Not Mail" list | | | | | | | | | | | | | | |
| # Catalog requests | | | | | | | | | | | | | | |
| Art and Assembly | | | | | | | | | | | | | | |
| Filing status | | | | | | | | | | | | | | |
| Credit card declines | | | | | | | | | | | | | | |
| Pending orders/credit card problems | | | | | | | | | | | | | | |
| "Hold" orders | | | | | | | | | | | | | | |
| Back Order Cards up to date | | | | | | | | | | | | | | |
| Cross-sales report | | | | | | | | | | | | | | |
| Customer Survey Card "follow-up" | | | | | | | | | | | | | | |
| Customer Replacements Returned | | | | | | | | | | | | | | |
| Accounts Receivable aging report | | | | | | | | | | | | | | |
| AR oldest Date | | | | | | | | | | | | | | |
| A/R >30 day level | | | | | | | | | | | | | | |
| Credit card problems resolved | | | | | | | | | | | | | | |
| Cancellations processed? | | | | | | | | | | | | | | |
| Y-connector used for training | | | | | | | | | | | | | | |
| A/R for media magazines | | | | | | | | | | | | | | |
| Refunds required processed | | | | | | | | | | | | | *continued...* | |

| Ship aheads up to date | | | | | | | | | | | | |
|---|---|---|---|---|---|---|---|---|---|---|---|---|
| ship address corrections done | | | | | | | | | | | | |
| Damage pick ups | | | | | | | | | | | | |
| | | | | | | | | | | | | |
| Status of Customer Service Issues: | | | | | | | | | | | | |
| All Customer Service Calls returned? | | | | | | | | | | | | |
| All Customer Service problems resolved? | | | | | | | | | | | | |
| Call tags up to date? | | | | | | | | | | | | |
| Damage claims filed on time? | | | | | | | | | | | | |
| | | | | | | | | | | | | |
| Other Accomplishments this week | | | | | | | | | | | | |
| | | | | | | | | | | | | |
| | | | | | | | | | | | | |

# Helpful Forms and Strategies

T his chapter is a compilation of forms and tips to help you run your company and get you to your ultimate goal. It contains many of the forms I used and referred to in earlier chapters. I have listed them here as an easy reference:

1. Dealing with the passive–aggressive employee
2. My crisis management plan (if the economy or your industry tanks)
3. Customer problem resolution strategies
4. One-call resolution (example of firm policy)
5. Employee management forms (write-ups)
6. CEO job description
7. After-the-sale job description
8. Ashton's sayings and other helpful thoughts
9. Employee bonus plan ideas
10. Contest ideas
11. Employee excuses

## The Passive–Aggressive Employee

The passive–aggressive personality is a real management challenge. These employees think you are out to get them. They want to get even. They want to teach you a lesson. In the movies, we call them the villain. They plot, talk bad, and complain behind your back, and they will drive you and your organization crazy.

The passive–aggressive person is not outwardly aggressive, but passively and sneakily aggressive with the goal of hurting. They don't want to confront you, and they don't want you to confront them either. Their spiteful tactics can destroy any teamwork you have built. They tend to act nice to your face and then rat you out to everyone else who will listen, or they make problems for you in an attempt to trip you up. Their favorite activity is to expose your flaws in public, especially in meetings. If you have a suspicion that an employee is undermining you, he or she probably is and is most likely passive–aggressive.

If you pay close attention, you will see the subtle signs and hear the subtle statements. I would record their words on paper so I wouldn't get angry at the time and give them the reaction they wanted. I would later play back their statements and gestures in a private confrontation. Sometimes they use sighs, roll their eyes, use sarcasm, or smile inappropriately. They will even use the silent treatment to get back at you.

Generally when you confront passive–aggressive employees, they act as if nothing's wrong. They don't want you to discuss the problem with them or fix it, because then they can't have their sneaky revenge. Therefore, it's really not a problem you can make better. Never underestimate its power.

Since you can only call them out on their behavior, you need good notes and actual examples. Look for these and write them down so you can read them to the employee when you sit down with him or her. My favorite is: "I have set up this meeting so we can work out the things that are bothering you about me so you don't have to go all over the office and talk about it. If we can't communicate on this level, I will be unable to work with you." Coach them on how to express their situation. If they use the silent treatment, you simply have to ignore them for the time being.

If one employee is making another employee particularly upset or angry, the employee causing this reaction is probably passive–aggressive. Never ignore passive–aggressive behavior. Always confront it after you get the facts. These employees will most certainly test your limits. Companies are much better off without these people, so if they don't change, get rid of them.

## My Crisis Management Plan

Since my husband is a worrier, I decided to develop a crisis management plan to placate him, never thinking that I would actually have to implement all three stages of it. I had my consultant help me complete these when he came onboard. Here is what I had in each stage. Laying out the plan in orderly stages also helped lower the stress levels of my managers during bad times because they knew there was an organized plan and not a string of continuous layoffs. We went to Code Yellow in November 2008, Code Orange in January 2009 and Code Red in March 2009.

**Code Yellow Plan** (if stock market drops 20 percent or more and stays there for three weeks or more):

No overtime (except outlet sale);

Reduce staff by 20 percent;

Hiring freeze (applies to all positions; possibly move people around);

Postpone all stock POs for 30 days;

Collect all payments for special orders up front;

Retail store special orders will be nonrefundable (including rugs);

Retail stores to sell out of stock only (include warehouse stock) unless top management allows exceptions;

Change HVAC setting 2 degrees;

Reuse price tags, packing, copy paper, etc.;

Offer employee option to pause 401K plan;

Zero spending, including office supplies (except copy paper, receipt paper), donations, display expense, computer expense (except with written approval from CEO or CFO), maintenance, equipment purchases, packing supplies, staff functions, etc.;

Landscaping to be done by employees;

E-mail invoices, receipts, and A/R statements to minimize postage;

Pause pay-per-click campaign and increase free online social media marketing efforts;

Save every sale (use win-win);

Request rent reductions or look at less expensive options;

Cease security officers temporarily.

**Code Orange Plan** (Applies when management and consultant decide economy is not bouncing back):

Temporary wage freeze;

$100 bonus to anyone implementing cost reduction of $10,000 on annual basis;

Renegotiate (and bid out) all regular contracts (trash pickup, equipment leases & maintenance, supplies, etc.);

Maintain all proven advertising expenditure;

Implement bonuses and contests to move in-stock merchandise;

Pause public relations campaigns for a quarter;

Minimize or eliminate outside contractor hours (programmer, consultants, etc.);

Reduce/cancel on-order inventory unless on back order or top 10 or special order;

All stock purchase orders must be signed off by management;

Buy closeout merchandise from vendors to increase margins (when you have open-to-buy);

Enforce win-win return policy (see detailed explanation);

Absolutely no spending unless top manager signs off on it;

Layer call center staffing in shifts (8–4 and 12–8) to reduce outsourcing costs;

Reduce salary expense by same percentage that sales are down, such as:

1. Reduce work force by one person in all departments with more than three workers;

2. Reduce weekly work hours and send people home early;

3. Reduce salaried employees' hours and pay;

Aggressively liquidate stagnant inventory (use e-mail, in-store sales, outlet store, Web specials);

Sell anything we don't need (including used cardboard boxes and pallets);

Repurpose everything for subsequent use, such as copy paper (use other side), printer and copy cartridges (get refurbished), price tags, all packing materials;

Go paperless (no reports printed).

**Code Red Plan** (final stage before liquidation)

Lay off rest of outside consultants;

No overtime, under any circumstances;

Reduce compensation, make additional layoffs, or reduce hours to decrease total payroll another 20 percent;

Lay off middle management and redistribute duties;

Continue hiring freeze;

Permanent wage freeze with new bonus plans;

Reduce advertising and marketing expenditures by one half;

Develop and implement new marketing strategy;

Require rent reductions;

Cut off computers and electrical breakers (except outdoor lights) at night;

Cut office and warehouse hours;

Put display windows on timers;

Stop all spending;

Eliminate all outside contractors;

Cancel all inventory orders except special orders that are prepaid;

Sell only inventory in stock;

Unhook one-half of the display lighting in stores;

Reduce insurance costs (by raising deductible, etc.);

Reduce postage by e-mailing receipts;

Eliminate association dues and subscriptions;

Reduce travel expense;

Reduce number of telephone/data lines;

Stop billing customers and require special order payment up front;

Reduce 401K plan matching contribution.

## Customer Problem Resolution Strategies

Here are some ideas on how to save a sale and how to resolve angry-customer situations.

### Win-win return policy:

1. Find out why the customer needs to return the item.
2. Offer alternative solutions (special order, e-mail discount, layaway plan, similar yet less expensive product, product alteration, etc.) to solve the problem.
3. Find a way to "save the sale."

### Win-win customer problem resolution policy:

1. Let customers talk until they have satisfactorily explained their problem to you.
2. Apologize.
3. Let them know the company's constraints.
4. Ask them what they feel is the best solution.
5. Find a common ground.

## One-Call Resolution Policy

Shades of Light has set a standard of serving the customer's needs with one call or e-mail. We require employees to research and find a solution to any request from a customer and follow up with the customer the day of the call/e-mail, even if it is to say that a resolution is being worked on and to explain why a resolution doesn't yet exist. The employee is then required to get back to the customer with the resolution the next day.

If it happens that the customer contacts the company before the employee gets back to them, information about the incident should be forwarded to Ashton.

If employees have any issues with Shades of Light coworkers not assisting their effort to rapidly respond to the customer, they should notify Ashton and their manager.

Shades of Light is known for its excellent customer service and meeting this high level of expectation is of utmost importance (see Mission Statement).

## Employee Management Forms

Use the **Recognition form** so that employees won't feel that you only record the negative. Use the **Verbal Discussion form** to record every discussion on the job that isn't being done as you would like. These don't always have to be signed, but I do like to e-mail a summary to the employee (and blind-copy the personnel department for their personnel file). The **Coaching Opportunity form** allows you to put in writing what you and the employee decide will resolve the problem. The **Job Clarification form** is the last discussion before the **Final Warning**, so this one must be signed by the employee.

The **Final Warning** is a clear message.

Great job, _____ !

Thanks so much for
(Description of accomplishment):

_____

_____

_____

*Take a BOW!*

Photo here

Great job, _____ !

Thanks so much for
(Description of accomplishment):

_____

_____

_____

*Take a BOW!*

Photo here

Great job, _____ !

Thanks so much for
(Description of accomplishment):

_____

_____

_____

*Take a BOW!*

Photo here

## Verbal Discussion Summary

Employee: _____

Date: __ / __ /__

Manager responsible for report: _____

Misunderstanding: _____
_____
_____

Expectation: _____
_____
_____

Manager: _____

Employee: _____

## Coaching Opportunity

Employee: _____          Date: __ / __ /__

Manager(s): _____

Problem/Examples:                    Strategies for Success:
_____              _____
_____              _____
_____              _____
_____              _____
_____              _____

I understand the above plan.

_____

Date: __ / __ /__                    (employee)

Date to review the above: __ / __ /__

## Job Clarification

Employee: _____

Date: __ / __ /__

Manager: _____

Problem/Incident: _____

_____

Expectation: _____

_____

Action to be taken: _____

_____

I understand the above. _____

                     Date: __ / __ /__          (employee)

Manager: _____

## Final Warning

Employee: _____
Date: __ / __ /__
Manager: _____

Recurring Problem/Incident:

_____

_____

Correction Needed:

_____

_____

_____

Consequence if corrections not made:
                Termination

I understand the above. _____

                     Date: __ / __ /__          (employee)

# CEO Job Description

Strategic direction:
>Annual/semiannual goals
>Measurement and monitoring of above with monthly progress check
>Dashboards and monthly analysis
>New business opportunities (contract sales, web marketing, etc.)
>Set and measure sales and profit goals

Marketing/IT strategy:
>Quarterly meeting to review results, approve promo plans, etc.
>Weekly web marketing meeting
>PR and interface with media

Buying:
>Exclusive product progress, approval of designs, goals
>Approve catalog layouts and Web product selections
>Problem vendors and replacement-product status
>Review costs/retail markup and vendor negotiation
>Discontinued inventory liquidation plans/schedule

Personnel:
>Compensation and incentive plans
>Second interviewing all FT employees
>Escalated personnel issues

Manage CFO:
>(A/R, inventory, office management, financial, bank relations, insurance, employee benefits, credit card fees, payroll, taxes)
>Cash planning
>Internal controls

Call center manager:
>Costs, productivity, contests, cross-selling, training schedule

Purchasing: backorder levels, discontinued inventory levels, large inventory purchase approvals.

Retail: set sales and profit goals, review budget vs. actual, revenue increase brainstorming (contests, marketing), operations.

Distribution: goals, costs, timely turnaround.

Sign accounts payable checks.

Circulation analysis and planning.

Manage contract sales department leads, bids, sales and delivered orders.

Review payroll reports.

## After-the-Sale Job Description

Exclusive product design: Design, get approved, get manufactured, have photographed, price with highest margin possible, write copy, get on Web, copyright as necessary. Assist other product designers as needed. Minimum 20 new exclusive items per month.

Merchandise assortment plan: To help find new categories of product, fill "holes" in current product categories, and get them on the website to test.

Marketing assistance (quarterly marketing planning, offer suggestions as needed, social marketing (Facebook, Pinterest, Olioboard, etc.), blog writing, copywriting for website.

Problem resolution recommendations: Assist management in resolving product or customer problems as requested.

# ASHTON'S SAYINGS

1. Source the problem. Get to the root cause. Always. And then retrain or deal with the problem.
2. Make it happen.
3. If someone is causing you too much stress, get rid of him or her ASAP.
4. Life takes you where you are meant to go. Whatever happens was meant to be. Go with it.
5. How are we going to make this work?
6. Can we sell 100? (Test for new product designs.)
7. So you screwed up. Let's review what you learned and move on.
8. Don't spend energy beating yourself up; let's focus on how to fix it.
9. I know you can do this.
10. Three must-do-today things that will move my company (or my life) forward. (Always identify these

three items on your to-do list as things you must do before today ends).

11.   Never allow employees to miss "deadlines."

12.   We don't have "policies." You must work out a win-win solution with customers and your staff.

## And Other Helpful Thoughts

1.   Know (and be willing to admit) your strengths and weaknesses so you can get the help you need.

2.   Learn to let go and let employees do their jobs.

3.   Be clear about all your competitive advantages, and if you don't have more than one, strategize and develop some. Hopefully this is also your mission statement, posted in every location and referred to constantly.

## Dave's (my husband's) management sayings:

1.   You can't know problems unless you live them.

2.   You can't know inventory unless you sell it.

3.   You can't know systems unless you operate them.

4.   You can't know people unless you work with them.

"Your company should be an evolution to excellence through continuous improvement."

—Skip Harris
The Country Club of Virginia

"Don't ever get confused between effort and results."
—Tom Wallace, Director of Racquet Sports,
The Country Club of Virginia

# Employee Bonus Plans

Bonus for store managers:
Salary + Quarterly Bonus: 10 percent profit greater than $_____ per quarter (goal and bonus amount to be reviewed annually).

Incentive bonus for IT/website manager:
.25 percent of weekly Web sales over $_____
+ extra .5 percent of weekly web sales greater than $_____ (higher threshold) per week

2011 monthly bonus for buyer:
For any SKU (item) where the gross profit is greater than $_____ (use 1 percent of quantity of catalogs mailed) on any SKU for the month (returns will be subtracted), a bonus of $___ per item will be paid.
Delivered sales bonus:
1 percent of increase in monthly delivered sales (after returns) over previous year; Retail and outlet store and contract orders will be exempt from calculations.

Monthly bonus for purchasing manager:
Discontinued inventory: if discontinued inventory is at or below target on inventory meeting day, then monthly bonus of $_____
Good Stock: if current inventory in warehouse (at cost) is less than past month lighting delivered sales plus 20 percent (at retail), then bonus of $_____ would be paid.
Backorder level: if backorder lighting (at cost at the end of the month) is less than 8 percent orders taken, then bonus of $_____ will be paid. Contract orders will be subtracted.
These goals will be adjusted after six months.

Distribution manager quarterly bonus:
$____ quarterly bonus if all the following criteria are met:
Warehouse labor salaries (doesn't include production) are 3 percent or less of sales;
Total warehouse expenses are 6 percent or less of sales;
Damage claims are below .85 percent of sales.
Bonus will be paid the month following the end of each quarter.

Incentive bonus for call center manager:
Biweekly bonus: $_____ per week if weekly checklist is completed.
Quarterly bonus: _____percent cost savings under _____percent income for the quarter.

Quarterly bonus CFO and sales manager:

Quarterly bonus to be paid month following end of quarter—

_____percent of increase in profit from previous year (before administrative costs).

## Contest Ideas

All contests should be structured so everyone who performs well can win (not competing against each other for one winner).

Save SOL $10,000 annually and SOL has a prize for you: $100 cash.

1. Call center:
   a. Group contest: If sales are _____ percent above previous year and gross margin is above _____ percent, all staff will get $ _____ per hour worked. Contract sales are exempted.
   b. Salesperson with sales per hour >$_____, gets $_____ monthly bonus.
   c. Beat Your Average Sales Per Hour contest: If your sales per hour for the month are >$_____, a bonus of $_____ will be paid.

2. Lampshade Sales (or specific category) contest: A bonus of _____ percent of lamp shade sales for the month.

3. Any salesperson with sales >$_____ in the category of _____ will receive a monthly bonus of $_____ (also can do several levels of sales and bonus amount).

4. Save the Cancelled Order contest: Calculate $_____ percent of gross profit of any order you get from a cancellation (note reason for cancellation and items then sold on contest form).

5. Web Sale Page contest (2 for 1 sale): If sell >$_____ in sale product, get one paid day off.

6. Luck for a Buck contest: For every sale >$_____, you get to pick a "money reward surprise" from the contest bucket.

7. Upsell contest: $_____ for any order over $_____ (50 percent higher than our average sale)

8. Cross Sell contest: If your cross sells are greater than _____ percent, $_____ monthly bonus.

9. Product Cross Sells contest: based on category such as chandeliers and shades, bulbs, chain covers, medallions or rugs and rug pads.

10. Gift Certificate contest: If you get $_____ in gift certificates, get an extra day off (to raise cash at end of year).

11. New Customer Sales contest: _____ percent of gross profit from new customer sales for the month.

# EMPLOYEE EXCUSES

**Is s/he (the employee) lying?** (signs that employee or interviewee may not be shooting straight)

1. Avoids eye contact;
2. Often touches own face, mouth, throat;
3. Smile is not real (only in mouth, no glimmer in eyes, no crinkled crow's feet around eyes, suddenly stops, not synonymous with words or gestures);
4. May place objects (book, papers, etc.) between you and him;
5. "I didn't do it" instead of "I did not do it," or uses the phrasing of your question to answer instead of just saying no;
6. May use humor or sarcasm to avoid the subject;
7. Eyes look to the left.

Guilty employees get defensive. Liars won't face the accuser. They become immediately relaxed if you change the subject while the nonliar wants to get back to the subject.

What it really means:

1. The employee's "mother" calls and says employee is very sick and needs three months leave = he's in jail and it's the girlfriend calling.
2. Everyone is closing early because of the coming storm = I have a lot of errands I need to do.
3. She never responds to my requests = I feel jealous.
4. I got tied up in traffic = I'm late and I don't have an excuse.
5. I can't come to work because my grandmother died = check the obituaries.
6. My child is sick, my dog died, etc. = I'm going to the beach for the day with my friend.

7. I have a doctor's appointment for my back this afternoon = I have a 30-percent-off coupon at Kohl's and need to use it.
8. My alarm didn't go off = I have a hangover and am moving slowly.
10. I have another doctor's appointment today [the employee is dressed up] = employee is interviewing.
11. I lost my keys and got locked out of my house = I spent the night in jail for a DUI/DWI.

# Chapter 6

## Final Thoughts

I f you are blessed with ADD, you inherently possess incredible talents. You are active, energetic, and fun to be around. You are always changing course and coming up with new ideas and new projects, many of which are never finished. You are driven and thus you accomplish more than most people. You are willing to take risks and not let failures bother you—they just make you want to accomplish more. ADD is not a disability; it is an invaluable asset.

Our significant others may find it hard to live among our clutter, our constant change in direction, and our high-gear speed, but they love our energy (most of the time), the new things we introduce them to, and our passion for life.

If you do have ADD, the key is to force discipline on yourself in areas where you need it. Dedicate some time every week to review the ideas I have presented in Chapter 2. Put these disciplines on your to-do list, and make sure you check one off every day. Take five minutes every morning to revise your to-do list and reprioritize it. I wish I could say I do everything in this book, but even as I write this, I review my own strategies regularly and having ADD, I will always struggle with the challenges that go with it.

I would love to hear from you. If you have a great ADD story, please e-mail me or add it to my Facebook page or website:

www.ADDtoCEO.com

# MENTAL POST-ITS FOR ADD CEOS:

Learn to meditate. This will be extremely hard for you since it requires completely erasing your mind of all thoughts. I focus on a "blank blackboard." Meditation is the only way to quiet our minds (without medication) so that we can fall back asleep.

Use Post-Its to remember appointments, things to do, things to take with you. The inside of an exit door at home, the car dashboard, and the place at work where you leave your keys are all good places for Post-Its.

Set aside time every day to get organized. Use technology to help you stay organized. If you lose your phone or keys, there is a gizmo you can get that beeps if your phone is separated from your keys. Smart phones and iPads really can help an ADD person.

Keep only one to-do list and train yourself to keep it with you at all times. If you use paper, keep the pad on your desk attached in a special place or at the bottom of your computer screen. But even better is to use smartphone technology for this list. Then prioritize and use asterisks to indicate the subset of tasks that is reasonable to finish in that day. Keep your grocery list and gift ideas on your smartphone as well.

Set up one "mess room" with wall-to-wall shelves to hold all your projects, clutter, reading material, and other things you think you need. Find an unencumbered space elsewhere that will be for work only, not storage. Collect what you need from the mess room, bring it to the clean, bare workspace. Do your work, and then return all materials to your junk room. Don't let your spouse in this room. If your office looks like mine, train your assistant to escort all clients to your conference room, or any other comfortable area from which no one can see your desk.

Every time you become upset or angry about a business-related matter, write it down on a computer spreadsheet, rate it on a scale of 1 to 10 for overall importance, and then enter possible solutions. Believe it or not, this will actually help you to stay calmer and not hyperfocus on a small problem. Then come back the next day and decide which issues to address.

If you become upset in a meeting, take notes about what you are feeling and why. Write down the exact words that were said (for later reference). Hint: This is not an easy habit to form by any stretch of the imagination. But it's well worth doing.

Learn to grant yourself "timeouts" when you get upset or overstimulated. Go get decaffeinated coffee from Starbucks, take a walk around the block, or simply detour into the restroom. Exercise is very important to us ADD people. It helps calm us down and gives us time to focus.

Use your smartphone to set audio reminders. If you don't have a smartphone, buy one. If you don't know how to use a smartphone, have your kids or a tech-savvy friend show you.

Break your annual goals into monthly goals and the monthly goals into weekly goals, all with measurable results. Review these lists every week and every month (depending on the goal). This keeps you focused on the priorities you most need.

Take a pad and pencil to all meetings and lectures so that you can take notes and draw pictures to help you pay attention. I also used this for employee "chats."

Don't stay in a job that does not allow some creativity. You are extremely creative and will thrive in a creative environment.

Decide how much time each week you would like to spend on work, family, friends, exercise, chores, e-mail, Web surfing, projects, and downtime. Record it on an excel spreadsheet and then schedule your calendar. Review every Sunday evening. Try to remember to stop once you've spent your allotted time for the week.

Keep a running list on your home computer or smartphone of all your nonwork projects, adding to it every time you have a whim. Try to finish one (or let go of one) BEFORE adding each new one!

# How can you use this book?

MOTIVATE

EDUCATE

THANK

INSPIRE

PROMOTE

CONNECT

## Why have a custom version of *From ADD to CEO?*

Build personal bonds with customers, prospects, employees, donors, and key constituencies

- Develop a long-lasting reminder of your event, milestone, or celebration
- Provide a keepsake that inspires change in behavior and change in lives
- Deliver the ultimate "thank you" gift that remains on coffee tables and bookshelves
- Generate the "wow" factor

Books are thoughtful gifts that provide a genuine sentiment that other promotional items cannot express. They promote employee discussions and interaction, reinforce an event's meaning or location, and they make a lasting impression. Use your book to say "Thank You" and show people that you care.